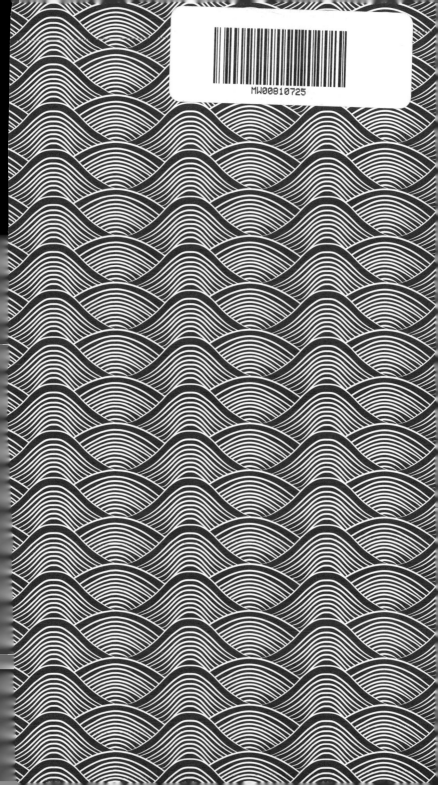

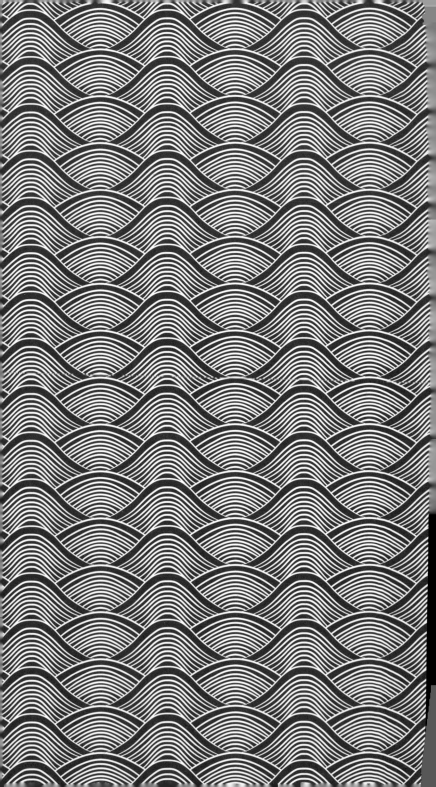

ABOVE ALL WAVES

富永
仲基

ABOVE ALL WAVES

WISDOM FROM
TOMINAGA NAKAMOTO,
THE PHILOSOPHER RUMORED
TO HAVE INSPIRED
BITCOIN

•

*Edited, with an introduction
and artwork by Paul Chan*

*Translation by
Yuzo Sakuramoto*

NEW YORK

Above All Waves: Wisdom from Tominaga Nakamoto,
The Philosopher Rumored to Have Inspired Bitcoin
2022

First printing

Published by Badlands Unlimited LLC.

Special thanks to Carol Greene, Jeffrey Rowledge, Martha Fleming-Ives,
Zhiwei Chen and everyone at Greene Naftali Gallery.

Editor: Paul Chan
Translator: Yuzo Sakuramoto
Line editor: Claudia La Rocco
Copyeditor: Damara Atrigol Pratt
Lead researcher: Lisa Yin Zhang
Research assistant: David Tavarez
Book design and cover art: Paul Chan

Paper book distributed in the Americas by:
ARTBOOK | D.A.P.
75 Broad Street, Suite 630
New York, NY 10004
www.artbook.com

Paper book distributed in Europe by:
Buchhandlung Walther König
Ehrenstrasse 4
50672 Köln
www.buchhandlung-walther-koenig.de

Contents

List of Artworks

Above All Waves:
An Introduction

Paul Chan

Only outsiders produce new ideas. Why this is the case may stem from how adherence to traditions and conventions typically sustains a field or profession: those who belong have nothing to really gain from doing things differently, if they wish to continue belonging. This is a story about an outsider who did not belong anywhere in particular, and what he, she, or they made, and how this outsider is rumored to have been inspired by the radical ideas of another outsider who lived three hundred years ago.

On October 31, 2008, someone going by the name of Satoshi Nakamoto published a technical paper entitled "Bitcoin: A Peer-to-Peer Electronic Cash System" to an online cryptography mailing list.[1] Cryptography is the art of securing communication between two parties. For instance, cryptography is what enables sensitive information like financial data to be transmitted securely when one buys anything online. In this paper, Satoshi proposed a new cryptographically-oriented digital currency system that did not rely on third parties like banks to keep track of its transactions. Satoshi's system was "peer-to-peer," a type of networking structure similar to older file sharing systems like Napster and BitTorrent. A peer-to-peer network is decentralized, meaning there is no central server that manages the network: each participant acts as a server by hosting the data being shared to the entire network. This configuration allows participants to freely join or leave the network at any time without affecting the integrity or availability of the data.

The data participants share on the bitcoin network is a file that acts like a digital ledger, one that is both continuously and systematically updated and transparent, open for anyone to see. This public ledger, which is the heart of Bitcoin, became known later as the blockchain. The blockchain is essentially a database that records every transaction that has ever taken place on the bitcoin network. Bitcoin being decentralized means anyone who takes part could own a copy of that blockchain. There is no central authority overseeing the blockchain or policing who could join the network. Satoshi proposed incentives for participants who take part in maintaining the bitcoin network. Special participants, called "miners," undertake an intensive computational process called "proof-of-work," which upholds the integrity of the entire system. Miners record transactions and verify the legitimacy of those transactions for a chance to be rewarded with the currency itself. Cryptography is what ultimately securitizes bitcoin. It ensures the blockchain is tamper-proof. Cryptographic protocols govern the most essential aspects of Bitcoin, which is why it is called a cryptocurrency.

In January 2009, about two months after the publication of the technical paper, Satoshi released the bit-coin source code for others to test and develop. The first recognized bitcoin purchase occurred on May 22, 2010: two large pizzas for 10,000 bitcoins.[2] About a year later, on April 23, 2011, Satoshi sent an email to the developers working on improving the bitcoin code base.[3] Satoshi wrote that he, she, or they were "moving on to other things." No one has heard from Satoshi since.

Rumor

The person (or people) behind the pseudonym Satoshi Nakamoto remains a mystery to this day. Over the years theories have appeared about Satoshi's real identity. A few people have even publicly claimed to be Bitcoin's inventor. But no definitive proof has arisen. In 2015, a new rumor began to circulate in online posts and press coverage of Bitcoin: that the name Satoshi Nakamoto was inspired at least in part by an obscure and largely forgotten "merchant" philosopher from eighteenth-century Japan named Tominaga Nakamoto.

These rumors have never been substantiated. Satoshi never directly mentions Tominaga in any of the online correspondences publicly available at this time. And even though reputable publications like *London Review of Books*,[4] *The Economist*,[5] and *The Guardian*[6] have cited the link between Tominaga and Satoshi, they chiefly rely on anonymously leaked documents and references by Craig Wright, a controversial Australian computer scientist and businessman who since 2016 has maintained that he created Bitcoin.[7]

This book offers no new evidence that Satoshi was

inspired by Tominaga beyond the story of Tominaga's life and his own words. As the reader will see, it is not hard to grasp how Tominaga's most vital insights align with the central ideas that make Bitcoin so remarkable. Still, like Satoshi's real identity, the relationship that binds Satoshi and Tominaga remains speculative. *Above All Waves* attempts to find value in this relationship even though (and perhaps because) its veracity may turn out to be demonstrably false. What might a rumor tell us? What value does it hold beyond its relationship to facts? If the story of Satoshi Nakamoto remains untold, then perhaps the story of the life and ideas of Tominaga Nakamoto can shed light on the intellectual, political, and cultural milieu that would consider him a worthy inspiration for something as radical and provocative as Bitcoin.

Commoners

Tominaga Nakamoto lived a brief and astonishing life. He was born in 1715 in Osaka. His meteoric rise within the ranks of the Japanese intellectual community was only eclipsed by his swift and tragic downfall, due in no small part to his radical ideas, once described by historian Tetsuo Najita as "appallingly disrespectful."[8]

Tominaga was the son of a successful merchant who helped establish a school of higher learning called the Kaitokudō Merchant Academy of Osaka, located in the center of the city. He enrolled in the academy at an early age; the few records that exist testify to his talent and discipline as a student. At fifteen, he published his first work, *Setsuhei*, which translates as "a critical discernment of doctrines." The doctrines in question were the classical texts from the dominant moral-philosophical tradition at the time in Japan: Confucianism. Tominaga argues that, without exception, those texts do not teach timeless lessons about how to be virtuous, because they are not even moral. Tominaga openly questions the doctrines and values the Kaitokudō held as sacred.

This would be the first of Tominaga's many transgressions. His ideas evolved from a set of views on language and history into a strikingly contemporary philosophical position that fundamentally sought to decentralize where moral values originate. He touched a raw nerve in the intellectual world in Japan, and was eventually considered so dangerous that he was kicked out of the Kaitokudō. Even though he continued to write and publish, Tominaga, who suffered from some kind of chronic illness throughout his life, never recovered from his exile.[9] His works were destroyed. Even in death he was *persona non grata*: his grave does not appear at his family's burial ground.[10]

The twentieth-century philosopher Theodor Adorno suggests that to truly understand any philosophy, one must know what or who that philosophy is arguing against. It is nearly impossible to comprehend a philosophy solely from within that philosophy. One needs to develop an understanding of the wider intellectual context in which it is situated. The Kaitokudō is that context for Tominaga.

The Kaitokudō was founded in 1726. Of the handful of schools in Osaka, it was one of the most well regarded. The classical ideographs forming its name translate as an educational institution that reflects "deeply into the meaning of virtue." In its heyday during the middle of the eighteenth century, the Kaitokudō was a thriving school open to all (men and women) but geared toward educating area merchants. The Kaitokudō benefited from visiting scholars who lectured on fields as diverse as poetics and history, and a good relationship with the city, whose officials understood that cultivating a vibrant intellectual community helped Osaka thrive.

A new world calls for new values to guide and nurture it. This was arguably the case in Osaka during the late sixteenth century, as it emerged from years of war to become a center of commerce and banking for the undisputed military victor: the Tokugawa shōgunate in Edo. Osaka became known as the "kitchen of the nation" during Japan's Edo period, which roughly stretched from 1603 to 1867. The city converted crops like rice to an exchangeable currency like silver and distributed goods to the rest of the country. It was said that 95 percent of the population were merchants.

The Tokugawa shōguns needed the merchants in Osaka to ensure that commerce functioned in an orderly and predictable manner. But despite their importance in the economic order of things, merchants were looked down upon, perceived as inferior people by the shōguns, the governing class of military nobles. In fact, merchants were considered the lowest class in Japanese society, akin to people with no real social status, and therefore not afforded basic civil protections, even though they essentially ran the country's economy.

The highly stratified nature of Japanese society during the Edo period all but guaranteed that classes remained separate and distinct according to the dictates of the shōguns. Lower classes were expected to obey without question these rulers of the country, who regarded themselves as being divinely endowed with wisdom and moral rectitude. Like others before them in world history, the shōgunate who waged war and conquered with might then appealed to a system of thought (whether religious or philosophical) to justify their rule. For the rulers in Tokugawa Japan, that philosophy was Confucianism.

Confucianisms

Confucianism arrived on Japan's shores from China as early as 108 BCE. By the third century CE, various Japanese communities had contact with the cultures and philosophies being produced in China. And by the fourth century, at least some Japanese were able to read and write classical Chinese, which is arguably why all early Japanese texts reflect broad Confucian influences and were written in classical Chinese. Confucianism's significance waned as Buddhism and Daoism entered the Japanese consciousness during the seventh century, and as Shintoism developed as an indigenous religion. Evidence suggests that as early as 700 CE, people were mixing Confucian ideas with Buddhist, Daoist, and Shinto concepts to create integrated forms of worship.

What is admirable about Confucianism as a philosophy is also what makes it useful as an ideology. The particular blend of spiritual discipline, social ethics, and moral idealism that Confucianism espouses was, from its earliest incarnations, meant to teach the nobility how to rule in a just manner. Like Plato, his contemporary in the West, Confucius wanted to influence the hearts and minds of political leaders and the upper classes of society—those who the ancient Greeks called the *aristoi*, which roughly translates, unironically, as "the best people."

Confucius and his followers belonged to the Chinese social class known as *shi*, whose members traditionally served kings in the Western Zhou empire as knights and counselors. After the collapse of the Western Zhou states, men like Confucius, who were knowledgeable about aristocratic rituals and traditions, became advisors to the competing rulers of the Warring States. Writings suggest Confucius himself held such a position for a short period of time, before entering retirement. It was Confucius's students, and their followers, who later shaped Confucius's teachings into a set of doctrines that became what is generally accepted as Confucianism.

According to Confucius, the three core principles that underwrite a good life are a commitment to lifelong learning, an emphasis on maintaining social relationships, and moral integrity in the face of fame, power, and wealth. If understood primarily as moral philosophy, Confucianism sounds like what one might expect from a model of self-cultivation. Confucius taught how to orient oneself toward goodness by possessing it in the form of "virtue" so that one can know *tian*, which in Chinese means "heaven," but also translates as what is absolute or infinite. The specific means for achieving this moral ideal was what Confucius's disciples like Mengzi and Xunzi and later generations of Confucian scholars would debate. But regardless of how their thoughts differed, these scholars never questioned the centrality of Confucius's writings and those of his main disciples: the attainment of virtue begins by studying these sacred core doctrines.

But Confucianism is as much a social mandate as it is a guide for individual self-transformation. The quest for virtue is not an isolated affair. For Confucius, maintaining familial and social relationships are decisive. A chain of association connects the notion of virtue to concepts like "order" and "harmony" and, ultimately, to the well-being of a society at large. Confucianism encourages ways of grasping this dynamic by using analogies that emphasize how a social order must be governed like a family if it is to function at all. This means that for Confucians, obedience to the fatherly members who run the family, and to the ancestors who brought the family into existence, are integral to how virtue is attained. The Confucian text *Classic of Filial Piety (Xiaojing)* is an exemplary instance of this common notion in Confucianism. From the first chapter: "Now filial piety is the root of all virtue, and the stem out of which grows all teachings. . . . It commences with the service of parents; it proceeds to the service of the ruler; it is completed by the establishment of oneself."

It doesn't take much imagination to see how a moral philosophy that considers obeying the "wisdom" of rulers a virtue would be valuable to authoritarian leaders and ruling classes alike. This is the case during the Edo period in Japan, when a resurgence of interest in Confucianism swept over Japan with the Tokugawa shōgunate's political assent. Generally referred to as Neo-Confucianism, this philosophy fused elements of Buddhism with the core Confucian doctrines. Neo-Confucianism's popularity was perhaps due to how easily it fit within Tokugawa rule, which prized a rigid social hierarchy and a centralization of power to shape Japan's fortunes that benefited the very few. This concentration of power and wealth also extended to morality. As the ruling class in Japan, members of the Tokugawa shōgunate considered themselves—and expected others to consider them—exemplars of virtue.

Living People

This was the philosophical and political environment Tominaga was born into as a *chōnin*, or a member of the lowly merchant class. Needless to say, just because one is denied the right to participate in politics or philosophy does not mean one does not have ideas about them. The establishment of the Kaitokudō was just one manifestation of the burgeoning understanding merchants had about their place in society, and what they could meaningfully contribute beyond their class-based responsibilities.

Their emerging class consciousness coalesced around the concept of "virtue." As mentioned before, the Kaitokudō was founded with the explicit purpose of reflecting on the deep meaning of this idea, braiding together political, economic, and philosophical concerns that allowed "commoners" like the chōnin to develop ways of thinking that did not rely on the wisdom of authorities. The scholars and students at the Kaitokudō were developing a concept of "virtue" as a moral guide for themselves as they sought a greater meaning and purpose in their lives.

This struggle to define virtue outside the bounds

of a ruling class did not begin with the Kaitokudō. Philosophers of an earlier generation, including Itō Jinsai (1627–1705), Kaibara Ekken (1630–1714), and to a lesser extent, Ogyū Sorai (1666–1728),[11] played decisive roles in amplifying similar ideas. Itō, for instance, believed virtue was a universal human value, and not subject to distinctions between "high" and "low"—in other words, between those who rule and those who are ruled. Itō grounded his interpretation of Confucian texts with this outlook and called virtue a "shared potential" that common people unequivocally had the capacity and right to claim for themselves.[12] Kaibara devoted his life to systematically documenting and studying Japan's fauna and minerals. He was known as the "Aristotle of Japan" for using scientific methods to catalog Japan's natural history. What Kaibara passed on to later generations was an intellectual framework where knowledge is best gained through careful and systematic observation. Kaibara's scientific work underpinned his moral vision, in which all human beings had the capacity to know objective things and order them in a principled manner as a means to improve their own lives. Like Itō Jinsai, Kaibara's message was that there was no need to wait for help from dominant classes or self-described wise rulers.[13]

Tominaga's most vital insights were directly inspired by these philosophers he likely studied at the Kaitokudō. But what fundamentally made his thinking unique, even dangerous, was how he positioned those earlier thoughts into relation with one another like stars in a constellation, creating a novel system of thought. Like Itō, Tominaga affirmed the importance of studying the ancient Confucian classics. But he did not consider these doctrines to be sacrosanct. Instead, he analyzed them like intellectual specimens from the distant past in the same way Kaibara studied native plants across rural Japan. By treating Confucian texts as objects of study rather than artifacts of reverence, Tominaga was able to critically assess their worth as moral and philosophical guides for those living in the historical present.

For Tominaga, what was thought and done before was not beyond criticism, no matter how sacred. This is what makes Tominaga so accessible to contemporary readers: he secularizes moral and political thought and places a premium on the needs of living people, especially commoners like himself, as an indispensable aspect of how to grasp any philosophy, political program, or religion. Tominaga is also insistent on highlighting how cultural differences shape the personality of individuals, if one wants to genuinely understand the ideas those individuals produce. His philosophy was unique within the intellectual history of the Edo period, and can be characterized as a kind of radical empiricism. For Tominaga, lived experience centers a philosophy truly worth believing in.

It is remarkable how advocating for something as basic as the right of living people to affirm and value their own experiences can cause so much fear and loathing. Tominaga's first important work, *Setsuhei*, only exists as a summary because he mentions it in a later work. Like much of his incendiary writings, copies of *Setsuhei* were most likely destroyed by the Kaitokudō. If his work was known at all, it was through rumors. The handful of writings that survived include *Writings of an Old Man (Okina no fumi), Words after*

Enlightenment (Shutjukō kōgo), and a treatise on music entitled *Gatkuritsu kō*.

Tominaga relentlessly criticized ancient doctrines purporting to embody timeless moral values. Beginning with *Setsuhei*, he argues that historical texts do not originate ex nihilo, out of nothing; rather, the sages of the past were competing against rivals to win the hearts and minds of people in their own times, composing works in order to gain intellectual supremacy. According to Tominaga, one can discern within ancient texts certain ways of writing that heighten their persuasive qualities. But in deploying aesthetic embellishments and effects to make their texts sound more attractive and powerful, the sages ended up misrepresenting the very traditions they claimed were timelessly true.

Tominaga argues that all of the major moral doctrines in Japan were guilty of committing the same fraud. In his first work, he levels the charges against Confucianism. In *Words after Enlightenment*, published in 1745, he focuses his polemical attack on the entire history of Buddhism. Tominaga contends that after the historical Buddha founded his core ideas, it is said that he conveyed them to his disciples before his death. Shortly thereafter, disagreements erupted about the meanings behind what the Buddha had said. Sectarian lines formed, with each sect using questionable arguments and claims to try to outdo each other as they fought to be the one true lineage of the Buddha.

In other words, the history of moral ideas does not consist of divine pronouncements from sages transmitting what is true through the ages. It is rather the story of ambitious struggles over intellectual and moral dominance, and how these struggles produce falsifications and exaggerations that render those philosophies utterly unreliable as stable sources of moral authority. Tominaga believed teaching these doctrines as if they are unimpeachable truths amounts to fraud—intentionally misleading and deceiving well-meaning people who are just trying to live.

In *Writings of an Old Man*, perhaps Tominaga's greatest work, his criticism of Confucianism and Buddhism extends to an attack against Shintoism, Japan's only indigenous religion. Tominaga argues that Shintoism did not originate from a "divine antiquity" as it claimed. The original Shinto doctrines were derived from combining elements of Confucianism and Buddhism in ways that people in Japan at the time found suitable and convenient. Factions emerged afterwards purporting to represent the true Shinto way, all competing for superiority under the pretense of teaching the people. This is why Tominaga found it foolish to seek fixed and timeless moral norms like virtue in any of the ancient doctrines. Each in their own way was in essence a history of deception.

The main thrust of Tominaga's criticism seems clear enough. But what is remarkable is how his philosophy also encompasses a kind of "critical aesthetics." In analyzing different traditions and doctrines, Tominaga recognized how they used certain "patterns of speech" to amplify emotional power in their language. He began to grasp how the sectarian conflicts that led to so many layers of distortion within a tradition did not occur haphazardly. There were rhythms to the manipulation. So for Tominaga, the role of a true philosopher is not to endorse the moral norms the ancient texts tried to convey, but to reveal the extent to which these "patterns of speech" were used as aesthetic devices to make those doctrines sound more compelling and more worthy of being true.

Broadly speaking, aesthetics is the domain that grapples with what it means to experience something agreeable (or disagreeable) to our senses. The search for beauty is what typically motivates aesthetic thinking. But Tominaga suggests that aesthetics can be practiced another way: by understanding language as a medium of expression as much as a transmitter of knowledge, Tominaga catalogs the techniques and tricks those doctrines used to magnify and strengthen their own aesthetic qualities. Although Tominaga does not formulate a comprehensive theory of language, he nevertheless creates an intellectual framework where aesthetics have the capacity to offer insights well beyond the domain of art. Tominaga considers the practice of aesthetics a form of political vigilance.

In *Words after Enlightenment*, Tominaga describes five basic aesthetic "patterns" observable throughout the ancient doctrines.[14] The first is *chō haru*, or expansiveness. This pattern describes a term that typically has a physical context taking on an otherworldly significance. In Shintoism, for instance, the reference to a physical terrain called the "high plains" is expanded to mean the divine realm of the gods, and the source of spirituality in all things. The second pattern is *han*, or metaphysicality, referring to the claim that a divine essence is responsible for the existence of all living things, even though the essence itself cannot be perceived in the empirical world because it transcends time and space. The third is related to han and can be described as "spiritualization," where the aforementioned divine essence manifests inside an individual and "blesses" them in some way. This pattern is used to create hierarchies that separate the wise from the vulgar by elevating those who follow the "true tradition." The fourth pattern, which Tominaga also calls *han*, is the use of ironic opposites. Here, terms are twisted to mean something other than, or completely counter to, what they typically intend. It is meant to show how ordinary language cannot convey a tradition's true scope, and therefore one must enter that tradition to appreciate what is really being expressed. Tominaga refers to the fifth and last pattern in Japanese as *ten*, or transformation. Language here is used to reinforce what the "spiritualization" pattern tries to achieve but places the emphasis on the power of a tradition's doctrines as a generating source of change.

He matter-of-factly claims that moral assertions which deceive people by deploying these aesthetic patterns are not worthy of attention because they have no real basis in human reality. And since all of the major doctrines in Japan at the time exhibited signs of deception, Tominaga concluded that they must be rejected. *All of them.* This is what made Tominaga a heretic. He openly denounced every moral system operating in Japan at the time, especially the one the ruling authorities considered sacred, Confucianism. He then affirmed the capacity of common people to attain the only kind of virtue that was authentic to him—the kind that was earned from the wisdom of thoughtfully and patiently heeding one's own lived experience. He attempted to decentralize how moral value was generated in his society, and in doing so tried to return some semblance of power to those who have been subjected to the rule of others.

"The Way of All Ways" is how Tominaga describes his own moral vision.[15] This "Way" does not identify with moral absolutes or divine truths. It is found instead in how one conducts matters in ordinary, everyday life. "Virtue" here is not something one possesses, like an object or a title. It is instead a capacity—to be compassionate to others and supportive of oneself "in countless little ways," Tominaga writes.[16] He goes on to explain that one ought to be virtuous *not* because it is endorsed by tradition, or a wise sage, or some ancient text, but simply because it is essential to human life in the present. It makes human interaction more easeful and peaceful rather than violent and chaotic, which is intolerable, as we the living today know.

This shockingly simple and commonsensical moral vision holds another practical advantage. If one seeks virtue in the daily practice of ordinary life, and doesn't waste precious energy on time-consuming debates about the ultimate meaning of concepts underpinning dubious systems of thought, one can then pursue one's own intellectual or artistic interests. Tominaga has fellow feelings for artists and scholars of all kinds. In *Writings of an Old Man*, he advises, "Make the time, and become wise by learning the arts which benefit you most."[17] Tominaga understands the "arts" broadly, as inferred by his commentary on how even in the Buddhist tradition monks were encouraged to study an art like literature or mathematics. No domain of interest is inherently better than another. What is crucial is that there is simply time to devote to a pursuit that enriches one. The ordinary devotion to an art—like the practice of daily life—is how one genuinely attains virtue.

For this eminently practical and open-hearted moral philosophy, Tominaga was exiled from his community. His troubles began after his first work was published, leading to his permanent expulsion from the Kaitokudō in 1730. He worked as a tutor in different schools around the Osaka area and continued to write. Rumor at the time was that he had a wife and child. It is said that he joined a Buddhist monastery for a period, and that the scholarship he displayed in his criticism of Buddhist doctrines came from his time studying those same doctrines when he was a monk. A year after *Writings of an Old Man* was published in 1745, he passed away at the ripe old age of thirty-one. It is unclear to this day where he is buried.

Spirits

Tominaga had no disciple or successor to carry on his work after he died. A handful of modern historians and writers have kept the legacy of Tominaga's work alive, including sinologist and journalist Naitō Konan and writer Katō Shūichi . But within the history of ideas in Japan, he is largely considered an eccentric outcast, if he is considered at all. European and American philosophical circles have so far ignored his work. Perhaps it is fitting that Tominaga's sphere of influence is found in a domain more empirically minded and practical—just like his philosophy preached. When one understands something about Tominaga's life and work, it is not hard to recognize how he may have influenced the creation of Bitcoin. By reinventing how money in the twenty-first century works from the bottom up, Bitcoin resonates with the spirit of Tominaga's radical legacy.

The question of value lies at the heart of this spirit. In the case of Bitcoin, it is the value associated with what we call "money." Fundamentally, the value of money rests on the notion of trust. A US denominated one-dollar bill, for example, holds value because it is "legal tender," a currency authorized and backed by the United States federal government. This means its value rests on one's belief and trust in the authority of the United States to guarantee the legitimacy of the dollar as a medium of exchange. A currency that is backed by a nation-state is called "*fiat* money." Fiat is a Latin term that translates as "let it be done." Fiat money is money that is willed into being by a nation-state. All legitimate forms of money that function on a global scale are fiat money—or they were, until Bitcoin came along.[18]

Without trust, there is no value. This illustrates a crucial aspect about value in general—it is at heart socially derived, insofar as it is people who make things or ideas valuable, rather than the thing in itself. There is arguably nothing *inherently* valuable about anything. Value appears whenever there are enough people agreeing about what is worthy of *being* valuable. And the longer people agree about the value of something, the greater the trust they tend to ascribe to it. As the trustworthiness of a thing accumulates *over time*, its value builds, until it appears as if that value is a natural and inherent quality of the thing itself. But this is an illusion, in the same way that an insane person might point to the seemingly horizontal skyline as irrefutable proof that the earth is flat.

What cannot be readily perceived about a thing's value is how it is the manifestation of social trust over time. The ongoing legacy of a nation-state's legal and military authority is what gives people faith that the fiat money they use to buy goods and services will be recognized by others as having the same value.

Bitcoin puts into question who ultimately has the power to ascribe value to money in ways strikingly similar to Tominaga's questioning who is ultimately capable of attaining virtue. In both cases, a claim is being made: that forms of authority do not have a monopoly on deciding who or what is worthy of being "good" or "valuable." Bitcoin did not originate from the monetary framework that every country in the world uses to secure its currency. The fact that it holds monetary value at all is astonishing. To do so on a global scale while remaining independent from the control of any one governmental or corporate commercial entity is unprecedented.

How Bitcoin was initially created also resonates with Tominaga's work. Bitcoin is made of computer code. And if early accounts of programmers and cryptographers who inspected the original code are to be believed, one gets the impression that Bitcoin had virtually no chance of working, because the code was seen as inefficient, even ugly.[19] What is especially noteworthy about the early criticisms of Bitcoin was that it was considered not genuinely innovative. Cryptographers complained that it was made with components and techniques that were invented ten and sometimes twenty years before.

For example, bitcoin's data structure borrowed a great deal from a series of technical papers published between 1990 and 1997 by Stuart Haber and Scott Stornetta, researchers who proposed a technique for ordering data called "linked timestamping."[20] Bitcoin's data is also maintained using a method called "Merkle tree," which ensures the recorded transactions are not damaged or altered in any way.[21] It was named after computer scientist Ralph Merkle, who first published his idea in a paper in 1980. Bitcoin's proof-of-work mechanism took inspiration from a 1992 proposal by Cynthia Dwork and Moni Naor, the computer scientists who originally came up with the idea of adding extra computational workloads for every network transaction as a way to fight email spam.[22] Even the idea of an anonymous digital cash system is not new. In 1998, computer engineer and cryptographer Wei Dai published a proposal for "b-money," which describes protocols for the creation of a secure and anonymous currency system.[23] Cryptographic researcher Adam Back invented the digital currency Hashcash in 1997, first releasing it as a piece of software, then publishing a paper on it in 2002.[24]

Whoever created Bitcoin combined old ideas from previously disparate fields and synthesized seemingly unrelated technologies and methods in a novel way. Doing this required a capacity to set aside assumptions about how things are supposed to work. In other words, it took an act of imagination to envision how something new could be made out of what already exists and have it work in ways that nobody had ever thought possible. Longtime security researcher and writer Gwern Branwen offers a crucial insight about the fact that Bitcoin was made by combining old and forgotten technologies:

"Satoshi could be anybody. Bitcoin involves no major intellectual breakthroughs of a mathematical/cryptographic kind, so Satoshi need have no credentials in cryptography or be anything but a self-taught programmer!"[25]

This is a remarkable statement about an inventor whose creation changed the course of the global economy. The original source code for bitcoin showed that it did not necessarily require a PhD in mathematics, or economics, or computer science to put it together. There is no evidence that any governmental entity, corporation, or institution of research contributed to its initial development. Satoshi did not ask for any authority's help or backing to create Bitcoin. Satoshi just did it. Tominaga's pathbreaking intellectual paradigm was also synthesized from old ideas. He also understood virtue—like value—is attainable by anyone willing to pursue and practice an art. Tominaga, like Satoshi, believed a person did not need the sanction or permission of an authority to create something meaningful for oneself and others.

In ways that perhaps Satoshi could not foresee, Bitcoin's success may be its own kind of failure. The amount of electricity it takes for the network to secure the blockchain has dramatically increased with the rising number of new participants over the years. Bitcoin's energy consumption has such a large (and growing) carbon footprint that environmentalists fear it contributes to the climate crisis.[26] Virtually every major government in the world is struggling with ways to deal with Bitcoin and other cryptocurrencies. Some, like China, Iran, and Russia, have either outright banned Bitcoin or have legislations in place to deter its use.[27] At the same time, those same countries (as well as many others) are researching ways to update their monetary system in the wake of Bitcoin. The United States, United Kingdom, France, China, and Russia have all signaled their intentions to develop CBDCs, or central bank digital currencies.[28] Which is ironic, because Bitcoin's very existence is a testament to the idea that a money system does not have to be sanctioned by an authority to succeed.

Since 2008, Bitcoin has evolved from a niche invention into a mainstream financial asset. Institutional banks have begun to embrace bitcoin as a legitimate money form. Financial news networks provide regular coverage of Bitcoin and other cryptocurrencies, which number over six thousand as of January 2022. New technologies inspired by Bitcoin continue to emerge within and outside of the legacy governmental and financial entities that comprise the global economy. The price of bitcoin is scrutinized as closely as any stock or bond.

The idea that the true value of Bitcoin is reflected in its price is similar to the notion that the real merit of a work of art is bound by the price it fetches at an auction. This may be the case for those who appreciate Bitcoin merely as a financial instrument. It is certainly that. But it also seems self-evident that, like a work of art, its enduring success comes from how it uniquely embodies a set of ideas and ambitions that make it so much more than just another kind of money. There is a distinctive conceptual elegance to how Bitcoin creates value. It stems from a framework where anyone can participate, the data from the participation is openly accessible to all, and participants are incentivized to protect and maintain that data by the framework itself. In a sense, the virtue of the system is the value. By its continuing existence, Bitcoin shows what Tominaga philosophized: it is indeed possible to create something that embodies what is "good" for the daily practice of everyday life and to grow its value without the need for a central authority. Even if Bitcoin collapses tomorrow, the spirit of both Nakamotos will live on, as a reminder that it is never too late, or too early, to practice an art that redefines what is possible.

Rumor, Reconsidered

The rumor that Tominaga inspired Satoshi may be appealing because it lends a plausible intellectual and political lineage to an invention and its inventor so profoundly unbelievable that they seem to have appeared out of nowhere. But even though Satoshi's identity remains unknown, not everything about Satoshi is hidden in the shadows.

Satoshi was part of a community, however briefly—and like all communities, this community inhabits a culture, however informally, that is expressed in styles and conventions, identifiable especially by those who wish to belong. It is generally accepted that Satoshi was part of the cryptography community. Satoshi first published the Bitcoin technical paper on a cryptographic mailing list hosted by www.metzdowd.com, a long-standing forum devoted to "cryptographic technology and its political impact."[29] Releasing the paper enabled Satoshi to get feedback and to find cryptographers and programmers with similar interests who might be suited as collaborators.

The character of the community Satoshi leaned on and worked with reflects a number of qualities Satoshi also exhibits. Perhaps the most obvious is the high regard for personal privacy. Using pseudonyms is characteristic of the cryptographically minded, because they value the power to secure secrets and maintain anonymity as vital aspects of freedom. This is arguably why members of the mailing list were willing to lend an ear to Satoshi's ideas when the paper was first published, despite the fact that "Satoshi Nakamoto" had not previously participated in the forum (at least under that moniker). The paper drew attention for its technical merits. But the use of a pseudonym also signaled to the community that the claims put forth in the paper came from someone, or someplace, like-minded.

The name "Satoshi Nakamoto" also signals a certain style that the cryptographic community would have found familiar, a recognizable characteristic for those who self-identify with that community. "Japanophilia" is historically the term that describes someone not of Japanese descent with an abiding interest in—if not outright passion for—Japanese history, people, and culture. Today, the term used online to describe this characteristic is "weeaboo," or "weeb." And although weeb was originally meant as a derogatory term for someone with an obsession with Japan, it has also been taken up by those who may be derided for being a weeb as an ironic or even affirmative gesture.

Early Bitcoin participants exhibit aspects that one

might characterize as weeaboo. Computer scientist and cryptographer Nick Szabo, whose 1998 concept of "bit gold" is considered to be a direct precursor to Bitcoin, and was himself scrutinized as possibly being Satoshi, wrote openly about the need to learn from Japan's history as a way to bring about economic and political change in the West.[30] Amir Taaki, a well-known early bitcoin programmer, used the Japanese word *genji* (which translates as "source" or "peace") as part of his email handle.[31] Gavin Andresen, who Satoshi cited as the person who should lead the development of bitcoin's client software after their departure, writes online posts from his personal website with the domain name "gavinandresen.ninja." French software developer Mark Karpelès, who moved to Japan in 2009, became the CEO of the biggest bitcoin exchange at the time, Mt. Gox. Before an unprecedented hack in 2014 that saw Mt. Gox lose a total of 850,000 bitcoins, the exchange handled upwards of 70 percent of all bitcoin transactions worldwide.[32]

It is therefore not surprising that a rumor claiming Satoshi was inspired by Tominaga would spark interest and continue to draw attention. It fits the brief of what the crypto community historically identifies with, while enlarging that identification to include a largely forgotten figure in Japanese intellectual history—one which provides a new and provocative backdrop to Bitcoin. And there is another element to the rumor worth noting; it is how the persistence of weeaboo in Bitcoin's mythology expresses an essential notion that does not (or perhaps cannot) be represented solely by the complexity and richness of Bitcoin as an innovative piece of technology. This notion does not negate the accusations of cultural appropriation that could justifiably be lodged against Bitcoin's origin story, but it does offer insight into why the weeaboo persists in the first place.

This notion is that Bitcoin is more than software: it is an expression that represents a deep and profound dissatisfaction with the hegemonic nature of what can be described as Western political and economic life. It is not a coincidence that Satoshi released the Bitcoin paper less than a month after Lehman Brothers, one of the largest investment banks in America at the time, collapsed and filed for bankruptcy on September 15, 2008, heralding the beginning of what would eventually be called the Great Global Recession. Financial sectors around the world crashed. Five trillion dollars in pension, real estate value, savings, and bonds disappeared. Eight million people lost their jobs. Six million lost their homes. And this was only in the US.[33]

The last recession was not the only one, and will certainly not even be the last one. Economic collapses in Western-style market economies (of which the US is both representative and the most extreme) are not random, nor mere glitches in the economic matrix. They result from a predictably combustible mix of widening inequalities that concentrates wealth into fewer and fewer hands, banking policies that overwhelmingly favor those with the means or access to invest as a way to generate wealth, and financial incentives that prize economic growth through unsustainable amounts of debt.[34] In 2008, the catalyst for the recession was defaulting subprime mortgages. In 2000, it was the speculative dot-com bubble. In

1990, it was oil. Recessions are endemic to Western market economies because the forces contributing to such volatility are structurally part of the economies themselves.

As Tominaga professed, living becomes intolerable when life is violent and chaotic. And when even basic economic and social needs are not available due to the unpredictable nature of one's environment, the desire to seek out—if not outright build—alternatives naturally arises. Objects of desire are expressions of just such longing for alternatives, and are conjured in one's mind out of a synthesis of what is found in reality with what one wants that reality to be. To describe this dynamic merely as cultural appropriation does not account for how desire's distortive powers are also expressive of real and persistent impoverishments that can be so disfiguring, especially when the social reality one finds oneself a part of feels unworthy of belonging to.

The fascination with Eastern cultures within the Western imagination has a long and complex history. It is a story that arguably began in 30 BCE, when trade routes and lines of communication developed between China, India, the Middle East, Africa, and Europe. Cultures all along the route mixed and mutated as commerce flourished. Various forms of "Orientalism" also emerged to underwrite imperial and colonial ambitions in the East. This network of trade connecting the West with the East eventually became known as the Silk Road. Unsurprisingly, Silk Road was also the name of one of the most well-known and notorious online marketplaces that first accepted bitcoin as a form of payment. Founded in 2011, Silk Road is generally regarded as the first true "use case" of Bitcoin, proving that it is a reliable and decentralized form of digital money.[35]

Here and Now

A similar questioning (and questionable) spirit that informed Satoshi and Tominaga inspired virtually all aspects of this book. As its editor and publisher, as well as the author of this introduction, I confess that I have no expertise in any of the fields that *Above All Waves* relates to. I am not a programmer, nor a cryptographer, nor a financier. I was not academically trained in Japanese intellectual history. The drawings of Tominaga throughout this book, including the one on the cover, are based largely on my imagination. No one knows what Tominaga looks like because there is no visual depiction of him from history. So I made one up.

Yuzo Sakuramoto, who translated the Japanese and Classical Chinese into English for *Above All Waves*, is an accomplished translator with a wide-ranging intellectual background. But he had no real experience translating or working with Edo-period texts, and did not know much about Bitcoin before this book. His work primarily involves translating interviews and texts by artists and musicians who identify with certain traditions of the avant-garde in Japan and the United States.

Like Yuzo, I come from art. In fact, it was through art that I found Bitcoin. In 2010, I started Badlands Unlimited, a New York–based press devoted to publishing experimental yet accessible books about art and contemporary culture in digital formats. As part of my work, I was always on the lookout for new technological possibilities for publishing. I came across Bitcoin in 2011 and the notion of the blockchain quickly captured my imagination.[36] The decentralized nature of a currency that was not backed by any central authority was interesting enough, but what really fascinated me was how the blockchain functioned like a new kind of *publishing*. At its heart, publishing is simply the act of making information public. And what is the blockchain if not an innovative, ongoing form of publishing that records every transaction that takes place on the bitcoin network for all to read?

There is another meaningful connection between Bitcoin and publishing. Johannes Gutenberg is credited with inventing the first printing press in Europe during the 1450s, and, like Satoshi, Gutenberg synthesized the existing technologies of his day to create his mechanical movable-type printing press.[37] One of the technologies he employed was coin making. Gutenberg trained as a goldsmith and most likely worked at a mint in his hometown in Mainz, Germany. He learned to make metal punches to print on paper by first learning how to make metal punches to mint actual coins.[38]

If the connection between Bitcoin and publishing was what first got my attention, it was how Bitcoin reflected a certain spirit that kept my interest. Much has been made—and I suspect will continue to be made—about the illusionary nature of Bitcoin's value. The philosophical core of the criticism seems to be this: How can some nobody simply invent value for something out of thin air? Out of nothing?

I have no great insight about whether the value of Bitcoin is real or illusionary. What I do know is that there exists a field of endeavor that has historically tolerated, even encouraged, the act of making something out of nothing. That field is art. Artists in cultures throughout the world have made forms that become valuable in all kinds of ways, out of nothing but sticks, marks on a sheet of paper, paint on fabrics, dirt on the ground, detritus on the street, JPEGs, even air. I am not suggesting that Bitcoin is art. What I am saying is that making something out of nothing, and having some chance of it mattering, is the epitome of the creative act. The term "art" is typically used to denote what is left behind by those ways of making and thinking that we admire and find valuable. But art is not the only form a creative act can take.

Endnotes

1   Satoshi Nakamoto, "Bitcoin: A Peer-to-Peer Electronic Cash System," October 31, 2008, https://bitcoin.org/bitcoin.pdf.

2   Laszlo Hanyecz, "Pizza for Bitcoins?," Bitcoin Forum, May 22, 2010, https://bitcointalk.org/index.php?topic=137.0.

3   Satoshi Nakamoto, email message to Mike Hearn, April 23, 2011, https://plan99.net/%7Emike/satoshi-emails/thread5.html.

4   Andrew O'Hagan, "The Satoshi Affair," *London Review of Books*, June 30, 2016, https://www.lrb.co.uk/the-paper/v38/n13/andrew-o-hagan/the-satoshi-affair.

5   "Craig Wright Reveals Himself as Satoshi Nakamoto," *The Economist*, May 2, 2016, https://www.economist.com/briefing/2016/05/02/craig-wright-reveals-himself-as-satoshi-nakamoto.

6   Michael Safi, "Australian Craig Wright Claims He Is Bitcoin Founder Satoshi Nakamoto," *The Guardian*, May 2, 2016, https://www.theguardian.com/technology/2016/may/02/craig-wright-bitcoin-founder-satoshi-nakamoto-claim.

7   Craig Wright, "Satoshi Nakamoto," *Medium*, April 5, 2019, https://medium.com/@craig_10243/satoshi-nakamoto-a7c4cf21253e (for instance).

8   Tetsuo Najita, *Visions of Virtue in Tokugawa Japan: The Kaitokudō Merchant Academy of Osaka* (Honolulu: University of Hawai'i Press, 1987), 102.

9   Shūichi Katō, "Tominaga Nakamoto, 1715–46: A Tokugawa Iconoclast," *Monumenta Nipponica* 22, No. 1/2 (1967): 180.

10 Najita, *Visions of Virtue*, 102.

11 W. J. Boot and Takayama Daiki, eds., *Tetsugaku Companion to Ogyū Sorai* (Cham: Springer, 2019) (for instance). Ogyū was a controversial scholar of the Edo period, and also one of the most important. His philological work and ideas were central to the debates about the value and limits of moral cultivation. Ogyū was squarely against the idea of commoners being able to self-cultivate moral values to achieve some semblance of virtue. This is why even though Ogyū is an important intellectual figure during Tominaga's lifetime, his influence may have largely been as

a "counterweight" to Tominaga's development as a philosopher.

12 Najita, *Visions of Virtue*, 26–43.

13 Masao Maruyama, *Studies in the Intellectual History of Tokugawa Japan*, trans. Mikiso Hane (Tokyo: University of Tokyo Press, 1983), 61–67.

14 Najita, *Visions of Virtue*, 107–111.

15 Our translation.

16 Najita, *Visions of Virtue*, 116.

17 Najita, *Visions of Virtue*, 116.

18 John Lanchester, "When Bitcoin Grows Up," *London Review of Books*, April 21, 2016, https://www.lrb.co.uk/the-paper/v38/n08/john-lanchester/when-bitcoin-grows-up.

19 Nick Szabo, "What Took Ye So Long?," *Unenumerated* (blog), May 28, 2011, https://www.gwern.net/docs/www/unenumerated.blogspot.com/3ecbb-48879787f383ef10206358e0a14adf2f5dd.html. Nick Szabo described the early reactions to Bitcoin this way: "Bitcoin is not a list of cryptographic features, it's a very complex system of interacting mathematics and protocols in pursuit of what was a very unpopular goal. While the security technology is very far from trivial, the 'why' was by far the biggest stumbling block—nearly everybody who heard the general idea thought it was a very bad idea."

20 Arvind Narayanan and Jeremy Clark, "Bitcoin's Academic Pedigree: The Concept of Cryptocurrencies Is

Built from Forgotten Ideas in Research Literature," *ACM Queue*, July–August 2017, 20–49.

21 Narayanan and Clark, 20–49.

22 Narayanan and Clark, 20–49.

23 Wei Dai, "b-money," the website of Wei Dai, November 1998, http://www.weidai.com/bmoney.txt.

24 Adam Back, Hashcash, 1997, http://www.hashcash.org/ (for instance).

25 Gwern Branwen, "Bitcoin Is Worse Is Better," the website of Gwern Branwen, November 21, 2018, https://www.gwern.net/Bitcoin-is-Worse-is-Better.

26 Mark Gimein, "Virtual Bitcoin Mining Is a Real-World Environmental Disaster," Bloomberg News, April 12, 2013, https://www.bloomberg.com/news/articles/2013-04-12/virtual-bitcoin-mining-is-a-real-world-environmental-disaster; Elizabeth Kolbert, "Why Bitcoin Is Bad for the Environment," *The New Yorker*, April 22, 2021, https://www.newyorker.com/news/daily-comment/why-bitcoin-is-bad-for-the-environment (for instance). Questions about the environmental impact of Bitcoin arguably began in earnest around 2013. Debate continues as to how exactly to measure the size of Bitcoin's carbon footprint and the impact it has on the climate crisis.

27 Wikipedia, s.v. "Legality of bitcoin by country or territory," last modified December 7, 2021, https://en.wikipedia.org/w/index.php?title=Legality_of_bitcoin_by_country_or_territory&action=history. Reliable sources for a list of countries that have banned Bitcoin vary in size and quality.

28 Andrew Ackerman, "Fed Prepares to Launch Review of Possible Central Bank Digital Currency," *The Wall Street Journal,* October 4, 2021, https://www.wsj.com/articles/fed-prepares-to-launch-review-of-possible-central-bank-digital-currency-11633339800; "Today's Central Bank Digital Currencies Status," CBDC Tracker, last modified October 2021, https://cbdc-tracker.org/. On January 20, 2022, the United States Federal Reserve published its first research paper detailing how a central bank digital currency might work. In a speech on February 1, 2022, India's finance minister Nirmala Sitharaman announced the launch of a central bank digital currency by 2022–23 as a means to boost the country's economic growth. For an overview of other countries that are researching or launching CBDCs in the near future, see CBDC Tracker.

29 "The Cryptography and Cryptography Policy Mailing List," Metzger, Dowdeswell & Co. LLC, https://www.metzdowd.com/mailman/listinfo/cryptography.

30 Nick Szabo, "Learning from Japan," email message to *SPACE Digest*, April 27, 1991, http://cd.textfiles.com/spaceandast/TEXT/SPACEDIG/V13_5/V13_500.TXT.

31 Amir Taaki, "Re: World's First Bitcoin Lawsuit—Cartmell v. Bitcoinica," Bitcoin Forum, August 17, 2021, https://bitcointalk.org/index.php?topic=99225.0 (for instance).

32 Ben Dooley, "Bitcoin Tycoon Who Oversaw Mt. Gox Implosion Gets Suspended Sentence," *The New York Times*, March 15, 2019, https://www.nytimes.com/2019/03/15/business/bitcoin-mt-gox-mark-karpeles-sentence.html.

33 Adam Tooze, *Crashed: How a Decade of Financial Crises
    Changed the World* (New York: Viking, 2018); Michael
    Lewis, *The Big Short: Inside the Doomsday Machine*
    (New York: W. W. Norton, 2010). A film based on the
    latter and of the same title was released in 2015.

34 Tooze, *Crashed*; Richard Wilkinson and Kate Pickett,
    *The Spirit Level: Why Greater Equality Makes Societies
    Stronger* (New York: Bloomsbury, 2010); Lucas Chan-
    cel, Thomas Piketty, Emmanuel Saez, and Gabriel
    Zucman, "World Inequality Report 2022," World In-
    equality Lab, December 7, 2021, https://wir2022.wid.
    world/. For the most up-to-date research on the social
    and economic impact of inequality as of 2021, see the
    latter.

35 Colin Harper, "The Long and Winding Story of Silk
    Road, Bitcoin's Earliest Major Application," *Bitcoin
    Magazine*, October 1, 2020, https://bitcoinmagazine.
    com/culture/the-long-and-winding-story-of-silk-
    road-bitcoins-earliest-major-application.

36 Sarah Hromack, "A Thing Remade: A Conversation
    with Paul Chan," *Rhizome*, August 25, 2011, https://
    rhizome.org/editorial/2011/aug/25/a-thing-remade-
    conversation-paul-chan/.

37 Andrew Pettegree, *The Book in the Renaissance* (New
    Haven: Yale University Press, 2010), 21–25.

38 Pettegree, 21–25.

Note on Translation

The following English passages were translated from *Classics of Japan 18: Tominaga Nakamoto, Ishida Baigan* (日本の名著 18 富永仲基 石田梅岩), published in Tokyo by Chuokoron-sha in 1978, and *Tominaga Nakamoto's "Treatise on Music"* (富永仲基の「楽律考」), translated from classical to modern Japanese by Shoichiro Yokota and Kazuhiro Into and published in Tokyo by Sakuhokusha in 2006.

富永
仲基

国がちがっても、時代がちがっても、道は道にかわりがないはずである。しかし、この道の道と名づけられた言葉の本来の意味は、それが実践されるところから出た言葉なので、実践されない道というのは、誠の道ではない。

No matter the country and no matter the age, the Way is the Way, but it is vital for the living to practice the Way of all Ways. The ways that cannot be practiced are not Ways of Truth.

ところで、日本のむかしには、人に向かってかしわ手をうち、四拝するのを礼儀としていた。また枚手といって柏の葉にご飯をもって食べ、喪のときには歌をうたい、故人を泣きしのび、喪がおわると川に行って祓いをしたものである。

In old Japan, people with good manners greeted each other four times, bowing to each other as they clapped hands. Food was served on an oak leaf as an offering. During a burial people sang and cried over their loss, and when it was over they headed toward the river to observe the purification rites.

それはおよそ古代以来、道について説き、法をたてようとするもの
は、必ずそれぞれの主張に対して、それ以前の誰かを祖にかこつけ、
そのものの主張することよりも、さらに秀れたことを述べようと
する。これは、非常に歴然とした傾向なのだが、後代の人はみな
この事実を知らず、そのため幻惑されるのである。

It has always been, since ancient times, that those who teach the Way and make laws have tried to disprove their predecessors and justify their own doctrines by claiming allegiance to even older ancestors. This is a very obvious tendency, but later generations who are unaware of this fact naturally become misled.

また頓部の経典に「一切の煩悩、本来自ら離る。一念不生、即ち是れ成仏」などといい、あるいは禅宗で、「四十余年説くところの経巻は、すべて不浄なものを拭う破れ紙である」などといいだしたのは、これはすべての法を破棄して、さらにその上に出たものである。

In the sutras that describe how enlightenment arises, it is said that all unease disap-
pears on its own since nothing remains
fixed in the mind; that is enlightenment.
In the Zen sect, a saying goes that the
sutras that have been taught for more than
forty years amount to toilet paper. Obliter-
ating all other doctrines is how progress
is made.

10

一 ᐸ P ᐸ P 五 Q Ge f

ハ = D M P T # T L 五 S L m

V Ω D i V f N a

ところで、この誠の道というものは、そのもとはインドから来たものではない。中国から伝来してきたものでもない。また神代のむかしにはじまって、今の世に習い伝えられたものでもない。天から下ったものでもなければ、地からわき出たものでもない。

ただ、いま生きている人のうえに照らして、このようにすれば人も喜び、また自分もこころよくて、はじめから終わりまでさしつかえるところもなく、すべてがよく治まるというところから生まれたものである。

Consider this: The Way of Truth was not born in India. It did not come from China. It did not originate in the days of the gods and has not been handed down to the present world. It is not something that came down from the heavens, nor is it something that burrowed up from the earth. It is just something that came from the light of the people who are living now, and from the idea that if we do things this way, people will be happy, we will be happy, and everything will be fine from beginning to end.

いったい、大乗の教えは、当時多くの聖賢でさえ、親しく仏の言葉を聞きながら、それでもなお信ずることも、了解することもできなかったものである。それが後世に至ってかえって伝えられたとすれば、それこそ逆に疑わしいだろう。

The Mahāyāna teachings are something that even many sages of the time, while listening closely to the words of the Buddha, were still unable to believe or understand. That they were passed down to posterity makes them very questionable.

ところが、後世の学者はみな、いたずらに、諸教はすべて仏の金口より親しく説かれたものであり、阿難が親しく伝えたものだ、と思っている。ことに、これら諸教のうちにかえって数多くの分離と結合があることを知らないのである。また残念なことではないか。

However, the scholars of later generations have mistakenly thought that all those doctrines came directly from the Buddha's own mouth, that they were directly conveyed by Ānanda. In fact, they do not know that there are many permutations among these teachings. Isn't that a pity?

さて、諸教が興って分かれたのはみな本来、順次に加上したことによるものである。順次に加上するのでなければ、どうして教えが拡大し分かれようか。すなわちこれは古今を通じて教えがたどる自然の姿である。

18

Now, the reason for the emergence and division of the various teachings was originally due to the progressive expansion of the teachings. If the teachings were not added one after another, how could they be expanded and divided? In other words, this is the natural state of the teachings throughout the ages.

それぞれの学派でそれぞれ自分たちが命名した言い方を誦えてそれを伝える。

Each school of thought recites and
passes on its own style of expression that
it has named.

このことを知らないで、愚かな世間の人は、これらをすべて誠の道だと思って、自分自身まちがった道理を身につけ、たがいに道理が通るの通らないのといって争いごとをしている。これは見ていてまったく気の毒でもあり、愚かしくもあり、またおかしくもあると、わたし（翁）には思われる。

Foolish people fail to understand this. Each believe their teaching is the Way of Truth, reason in error, and fight each other about whether or not their way is right. I feel sorry for them, for they seem to me to be clueless and ridiculous at the same time.

それなのに、その秘伝・伝授というものを作った理由をたずねると、その能力が熟していないものには、すぐに伝授することが困難であるからだと答える。これにも一理あるようだが、ひたすらかくして簡単に伝授することをせず、また値段を定めて伝授するというような道は、すべて誠の道ではないということを、よく心えるべきである。

When you ask them why they shroud
their teachings with such pomp and
secrecy, they reply that it is difficult to
teach those who are not up to certain
standards. This argument may be sound,
but keep in mind that any teaching that
only benefits the few, is purposefuly
esoteric, and is taught for a certain price
is not the Way of Truth.

みなすべて見当はずれの間違った意見である。

They are all misguided and wrong.

わたし（仲基）は幼いころ、ひまであったから、儒教の典籍を読むことができた。そして少し長ずるに及んで、ひまがあったから、仏教の典籍を読むことができたが、これによって、「儒・仏の道もまたやはり同じようなものだなあ、みな善を樹立することを目的としているだけだ」と思った。

When I was a child, I was able to read
Confucian texts because I had free time,
and when I was a little older, I was able
to read Buddhist texts because I had free
time, and this made me think, "The
Confucian and Buddhist paths are the
same, they all aim to establish goodness."

儒教がひとに教えようとしているものは、善であり、仏教がひと
に教えようとしてるのも善であって、ひとに善を教えようとし
ている点では一つであるが、ほかのことはともかく、これらの教え
が世の人を幻説と文飾とに耽溺させるものであることをどう
したらよいか。

Confucianism teaches goodness, and Buddhism teaches goodness, and they are one in that they teach goodness to people. It is one thing to try to teach people goodness, but how should we deal with the fact that these teachings are making people in the world indulge in illusions and ornate language?

32

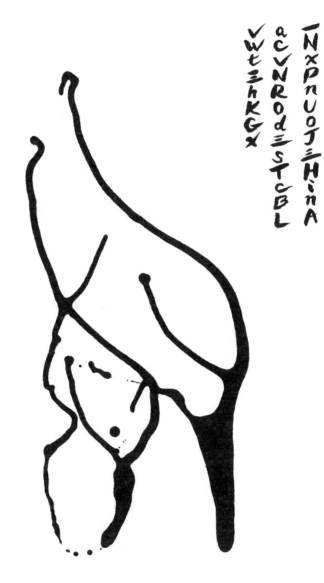

INXPNUOJEHINA
aCVNRODESTCBL
VWt=hKGX

33

いったい、言葉にはそれに応じた事物があるものであって、道はこのために分かれるのであり、国にはそれに応じた習俗があって、道はこのために異なるのである。

Each language has its own character, and this is why the Way is different. Each country has its own customs, and this is why the Way is different.

いったい、仏教に戒律があるのは、ちょうど儒教に礼があるような
ものである。　礼は、道が時に応じて制するもので、身体・言語・
意志のすべてに礼があり、これをほかにしては儒教はない。　同様
に、戒律をほかにして仏教はない。

Precepts are to Buddhism what rites are to Confucianism. Rites are something that the Way controls from time to time, and there are rites in the body, speech, and will, without which there would be no Confucianism. Similarly, there is no Buddhism without the precepts.

五戒は、もともと悪をいましめたものであるが、絶対に生きものを殺したり、酒を飲んだりしてはいけない、という意味であれば、それは間違っている。

The Five Precepts were originally meant
to condemn vices, but if they mean that
we should never kill living things or
drink alcohol, they are wrong.

はなはだしい場合は、菩薩は女に生まれることがなく、仏としての本性（仏性）に気づかないものを女性と名づける、というほどになっている。

It is said that a bodhisattva is never born as a woman, and those who are unaware of their true nature (Buddha nature) are called women.

人間が天地の間にあるかぎり、またどうしてただ女性の身だけを嫌う理由があろう。

As long as people exist between heaven and earth, why do we exclusively loathe women?

だからわたしは、かつて「およそ世の僧にして、もし仏が幻術をてだてとしたことを知り、世の儒者にして、孔子の教えが文辞によっていることを知るなら、そのときは、その道を修めて遅々とした歩みに停滞することはないだろう」といったのである。

44

That is why I once said, "If the monks of the world knew that the Buddha used illusion as a tool, and the Confucian scholars of the world knew that Confucius's teachings were based on literary rhetoric, then they would finally master the Way and not dwell on their dull progress."

儒者は、世のひとを欺瞞するものだと仏教をそしるが、みずからも類を等しくしていることを知らないものといってよい。

Confucian scholars criticize Buddhism for deceiving people in the world. But they themselves do not realize that they are also the same in kind.

インド人の幻術にしても、中国人の文辞にしても、日本人の直情にしても、これらはみなその習俗が、そうなのである。いたずらにその習俗をあげて、たがいに非難しあうのは、全く血気の勇である。

Whether it is the magical attributes of the Indians, the literary rhetoric of the Chinese, or the unadorned sentiments of the Japanese, all of these practices are the same. It is sheer bloodthirsty insolence to condemn each other for such practices.

いったい、月日のうつりかわりは、日月星辰の掌るところであっ
て、この理を知らなくても支障はない。かえってこれについて是
非を論ずるひとは、知恵の乏しいひとばかりである。

The changes of the days are under the control of the sun, moon, and stars, and there is no problem even if one does not know this truth. On the contrary, the only people who argue about this are those with little wisdom.

多くの規範（法）は互いにあい対応するけれども、要するに善を行うということに帰する。かりにも、その規範を守って、それぞれで善を行うことに熱意を示すときは、どうしてあれこれと選択する理由があろう。仏教も結構であり、儒教も結構であって、仮にも善を行なおうとするのであれば、それこそは一家をなすものである。

Although many norms (laws) correspond to each other, they all boil down to doing good. If we follow those norms, each demonstrating our eagerness for doing good, why choose this or that? Buddhism is fine, Confucianism is fine, but if you are trying to do good, then that is what makes us a "family."

真実、その志が善を行なうことにあるときは、どうしていけないことがあろう。いたずらに幻説と文飾とに耽って、善を行なわないもののことも、私は知らない。

The truth is, when our aspiration is to do good, what can go wrong? I do not care about those who do not practice goodness by unnecessarily indulging in illusions or ornate language.

いったい、善は行わなければならないものであり、悪はしてはならないものであって、善をすれば道理によくかない、悪をすれば道理にもとることは、天地本来の理法である。もとより儒・仏の教えにまつまでもない。

It is the original law of heaven and earth that good things must be done and evil things must not be done, and that doing good is in accord with reason and doing evil is against reason. There is no need to seek the teachings of Confucianism and Buddhism.

わたしは、儒教を奉ずるものではないし、道教を奉ずるものでも、また仏教を奉ずるものでもない。これらの傍に身を置き、これらの言行を観察しながら、ひそかにこのように論じているものである。

I am not a follower of Confucianism,
Taoism, or Buddhism. Situating myself
within their thinking while observing
their words and deeds, I secretly make
my arguments.

63

自分は音楽家なのでしょう。革や木を削り、つなぎ綴合わせ、また、金属や石、竹を加工し曲げておこなう弦や楽器の調整も、また、それらを巧みに操作して演奏する技術も、私はそれをするのに、わざわざ強いてすることはありません。

I suppose I am a musician. I don't have to go out of my way to adjust strings and instruments—by carving leather or wood and piecing them together, or by reshaping metal, stones, or bamboo—or employ techniques to play them skillfully.

尺度は信の集まるところ・・・・（信は徳の生じる母胎です。）この集まるところ、母胎が確立してはじめて、万物はそのあるべき所を得るのです。

Tuning the scale is how trust gathers. . . .
(Trust is the mother womb from which
virtue arises.) Only when this gathering
place, this center, is found, will all things
have their proper place.

およそ、人たるもの、音声を発しないということはなく、音声を発すればそこには音の高低が伴うのであり、音の高低すなわち音律があれば、そこにそれぞれの音律の名称も伴うであろう。

There is no such thing as a man who does not speak, and when he speaks, it is accompanied by the pitch of the sound, and when there is a pitch, or a temperament, it is accompanied by the name of each temperament.

「言に物有り」というのは吾が学問が立脚する根本である。

"There is substance to what is said" is the basis of my philosophy.

雅頌の声は（西土や古代のように）遠く離れたところにあるのではない。百姓が日々用いているその中にあることを知らぬだけなのである。

Music and rites are not derived from a faraway place (like a Western Paradise or ancient time). We just don't hear them from within the sounds of peasants simply living day to day.

INXPRUOJEHIN
AacVNRodESTc
BLVWtEhKGx

74

INXPNUOJEHINAQCVN
RODESTCBLVWTEHKGX

75

生活の場が異なれば傾向が異なり、傾向が異なれば好みや習慣が異なる。　社会の上下でそれぞれの音楽が異なるのは、現実から生じる自然な状況である。　したがって、それぞれの場について、それを求めるしかほかはない。

Different places in life have different tendencies, and different tendencies have different tastes and habits. It is a natural situation that arises from the reality that music from different social levels differs. As such, there is no alternative but to follow what each kind of music has to offer.

ああ、今現代にあって、古昔の真正の音楽を作ることができないのは、なぜであろうか。・・・・・（真正の音楽を）求めるには、人それぞれの場についてするほかなく、それにはその場の現実に反るほかないのである。

Oh, why is it that in this day and age we are unable to create the authentic music of ancient times? . . . The only way to seek (authentic music) is to do it in each person's own place, and to do that, you have to embrace the reality of that place.

いったい、言語は時代の推移につれて異なり、音声は時とともに上下するものであって、訛といわれるものも、ほんとうの訛ではない。いわゆる、言語には時代の制約があるからである。

The fact is, languages change over time, and how words sound rises and falls with time, so what is called an accent is not exactly an accent. Language is subject to the landscape of its time.

このように、古の先王の時代、雅頌の声を制定し、それによって民に道を教えた時代にあってさえ、男女の諍い、争闘、犯罪や訴訟は絶えることがなかった。まして況や、後世のそうした真正の音楽がない時代にはどうであろうか。ただ、この時代の民の愚かなる様子に、どのようにしてかこれを変えて影響を及ぼすことはできないであろうか。

So, even in the days of the ancient kings, when they established music and rites and taught the people the Way, there was no end to the quarrels between men and women, and crimes and lawsuits of all kinds. And how much more so in the later times when there is no such genuine music? How can we change and influence the foolishness of the people of this age?

世界の説は、その実は漠然としたもので、人の心のはたらきを語っているに過ぎない。

The theory of the world is actually a vague one, and merely describes the workings of the human mind.

空・有の説が論じられて久しい。

It has been a long time since the theory of emptiness and existence was discussed.

なぜなら、いやしくも、その身において善を行えば、それでよいのである。またどうして性に善・悪のどちらかを決める必要があろう。かりにも、その心において悪がなければ、それでよいのである。

For if one does good in one's own body,
then it is good. Why is it necessary to
decide whether sex is good or evil? If there
is no evil in the spirit, then it is good.

しかしそうではあるが、はたして何をもとに、いわゆる悪知恵でないことを理解するだろうか。そうなると、これはむずかしい。そのときは、達識の人が手分けをして探し求めて、その欠点を塞ぐことに期待するほかない。

No matter how true my claims are, how do I convince people that my intentions are not cunning? This is a difficult question to answer. In times like these, we have no choice but to hope that knowledgeable people will join hands to search for the flaws and fix them.

それは、ただ物事に対しては、その当然になすべきことをつとめ、

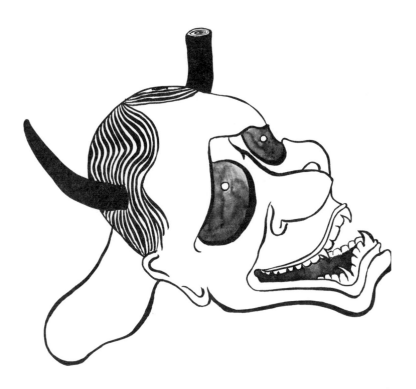

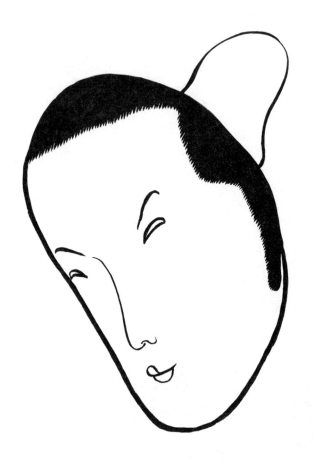

We should aspire to be profoundly ordinary
in all matters.

bc9tjylhtrcp八二元9√acf
a三g√d九七二∪九n∨r八五K七零XP

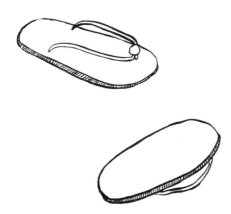

97

哀淫なるものに心を動かされるように、肉などの美味に身体が向かうことがあるかもしれないが、それらは一時口にすることはできても、恒にそればかりを摂ることはできない。それを食べ過ぎれば、病気にもなり肥満ともなる。人は皆、それが美味であることを知って、しかもそれを適度に節制すべきことを知っているのである。

Like our mind being moved by pleasures and sorrows, our body may turn to meats and other delicacies. But although we may eat them on occasion, we cannot consume them all the time. If you eat too much of them, you will get sick and become obese. We all know that they are delicious, but we also know that they should be consumed in moderation.

悪いものは食べず、たくさんのものを食べないことである。

Do not eat bad things; do not eat much
of anything.

楽しみごとにもおぼれず、悲しみごとにも自分を見失わず、

Do not wallow in what is pleasing, or drown in what is sad.

おおよそ古書を読もうとする時、皆すべて必ず、その書物の中でそれを解釈しなければならないのであって、もし仮に他書での言葉の意義をそのまま守ってそれによって当たるようなことをすれば、多くの破綻が生じる。

When reading an ancient book, one must always interpret it within the context of that book, and if one were to follow the meaning of a word from another book and use it as a guide, there would be many failures.

いったい比喩というものは、ゆったりとおおらかにこれを説いて、その意趣が成り立つもので、必ず全部が全部、いちいち結びつけなくても、それでよいものである。

Metaphors are meant to be understood in a relaxed and generous manner, and they need not be connected to each other for them to make sense.

またどうして道理としての空・有を考える必要があるだろう。いたずらにこれを説いて、たがいにやかましく攻撃しあうなど、すべて無用なことに属する。

Why do we need to think about emptiness
and existence as truth? It is useless to
preach about them and attack each other
in a furious way.

またわが身にあてはめて考え、悪いことは人にしないことである。

Strive to put yourself in other people's situations and do not wrong them.

愚かなるものをあなどらず、

Never underestimate the dumb.

人あたりがするどく、角のたつようなことをせず、なることなく、せかせかとせわしい態度をとらず、ひがんで頑固に

Do not be snide and mean-spirited, do not be misleading about people's motives or be difficult, and do not be a bully.

暇な時間のあるときは、自分の身にとって有益な学芸・学問を学んで、賢明になるようつとめることである。

Make the time, and become wise by
learning the arts which benefit you most.

今の文字を書き、今のことばをつかい、今の食物をたべ、今の衣服を身につけ、今の調度をもちい、今の家に住み、今の習慣に従い、今の掟を守り、今の人と交際し、いろいろな悪いことをせず、いろいろとよいことを実践するのを誠の道ともいい、それはまた、今の世の日本で実践されるべき道だともいえるものである。

To write in today's style, to speak today's language, to eat today's dishes, to wear today's clothes, to use today's tools, to live in today's houses, to follow today's customs, to abide by today's rules, to enjoy the company of people from today, strive to not do bad, but do what is good—that is the Way of Truth, that is how to practice the Way in Japan today.

願いとするところは、わたしが伝えるときには、さらにその人がこれを広く都の人たちに伝え、それからさらに韓国あるいは中国に伝え、それからさらにこれを西域の国々に伝え、それによってこれを釈迦牟尼誕生の地に伝えて、世の人をしてみな道において光明を見いださせることができれば、それで死んでも、朽ちはてることはない。

My hope is that when I tell someone this, they will pass it on more widely to the people in big cities, and then to Korea and China, and then to the countries in Central Asia, and then to the land of Shakyamuni's birth. So that all the people of the world may find light on the path. If this is achieved, even if I die, the idea will not perish.

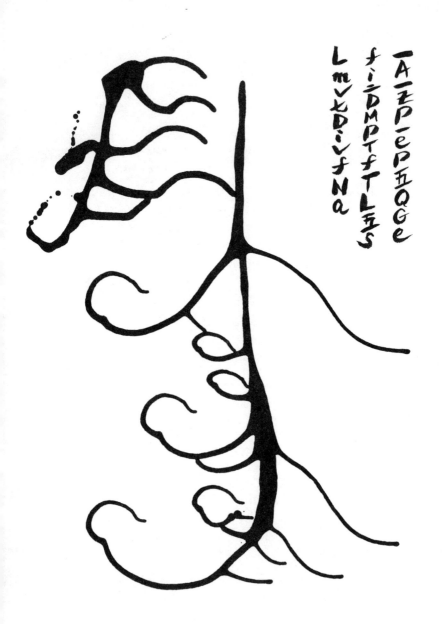

122

123

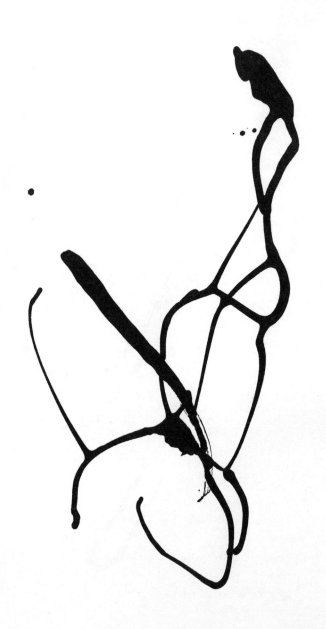

124

About the Contributors

Paul Chan is an artist, writer and publisher based in New York. He is the winner of the Hugo Boss Prize in 2014, a biennial award honoring artists who have made a visionary contribution to contemporary art. His work is in the collections of the The Museum of Modern Art, the Whitney Museum of American Art, the Guggenheim Museum, the Walker Art Center, among others. His press Badlands Unlimited was the first art book press to accept Bitcoin as a form of payment at the 2011 New York Art Book Fair. In 2017, Badlands created the Badlands Crypto Group and conducted workshops in New York to educate artists and writers about the risks and benefits of cryptocurrencies like Bitcoin.

Yuzo Sakuramoto is a translator and bookseller based in New York. He was co-founder of the music fanzine *MUSIC*, and has translated interviews with and essays on/by artists including Nam June Paik, Takehisa Kosugi, Jonas Mekas and Christian Marclay.

一五　七　三四五六　一

六　零　七　二四　零三七

零五五二七六六五

六四七七六五零六

四一五一二七四六

三七零零一六六四

四五零三零一五五

五一四六一三二七

四零六一四三四
二六二二六七七
二五六五七六一
一六六五零六
五五一六六五零六
六七零四零一七五
四七一三四五七二
四四二零三一四二
三五三一一五一三